I0490680

50 SHADES OF A PROJECT MANAGER

BY

William Layne

(A frustrated cowboy)

© William Layne, 2023

HOWDY

Howdy and welcome to my "posse"!!!

I have decided to write a book about what I have learned while managing projects over my many years in the IT industry. You may ask, why read this book, well if you don't read it, you will never know, but I think I have made my fair share of mistakes and hopefully I can help in preventing you making the same mistakes

This book is not a replacement for formal project management training, but is a collection of my opinions, gained from years of experience as a Consulting Project Manager (and a father) of how to manage people, resolve issues and deliver what the "customer " wants!!

When I was a kid, I would spend all of my free time reading cowboy books and playing "Cowboys and Indians" and I dreamed of becoming a cowboy one day

As I got older, I wondered what career I could take that would allow me to be like my childhood heroes, so I became a Project Manager and now I "herd people", and defend the customer, but I swear I did not shoot the deputy!!

This book is for all those unsalted PMs who having done the formal training, find themselves in the thick of managing a project, with all the complexities of the customer, your boss, and all other stakeholders to deal with….and you feel like you are in a stampede

Being a successful Project Manager is not about following PM methodologies, nor is it delivering to your project's targets of price, time, etc.

To be a successful Project Manager you need to be that person that people are happy to approach to have a chat, to help manage and resolve issues, motivate and drive your team and most importantly take ownership for the successful delivery of your project – You need to be a "People Person"

Although this book has been written from a Project Manager's perspective, many of the lessons and tips in this book can equally be applied to other job roles, including Account Executives, Service Management, Support and Senior Management

© William Layne, 2023

Finally, let me apologise NOW for the "way this book is written", I write as I speak. Sorry!!!

BILL OF SALE

Read the Statement of Works

Please remember to "READ THE STATEMENT OF WORKS". As Project Manager, it is important that you have read and understood the SoW/Project Brief, etc. Take time to read the SoW and understand the terms and conditions, milestones, acceptance criteria and roles and responsibilities

There is nothing more embarrassing than being in a meeting with the customer and claiming a fact about *your* SoW only to be contradicted by the customer

Also, if you haven't read the SoW, how would you know if you have deviated from scope, etc?

SoW risks and assumptions

SoWs will often have assumptions, customer responsibilities, etc.

As a project manager it is important to review these assumptions and either confirm (and close) or for any that cannot be closed, these should be added to your RAID log

Remember the famous saying about assumptions, if not confirmed they will make a "donkey out of you U and ME" and that's the polite version!!!

All those contracts…..where to start

SoWs are usually "backed off" by a Master Service (Framework) Agreement (MSA), in which the parties agree to most of the terms that will govern future work

Normally as the PM, you don't need to have read the MSA, but it is worth being aware of it, especially in the event of major disagreements / threat of termination from the customer

If you do find yourself on a project where the agreement of the SoW was complex or involved legal teams, then it may be worth during start-up, to have an internal call with your legal team to understand any key terms which may impact the delivery of the project

Get to know your internal stakeholders

It is really important during the initiation phase of your project that you have spoken to or had a handover meeting from Sales/Pre-Sales/Bid Team to the Delivery Team (don't have the handover without your SMEs)

One of the worst things you can do as a PM is to have a call with the customer to discuss decisions made during pre-sales and not be aware of what has been previously agreed. The customer will see this as an organization that is not "joined-up"

Engage the Pre-Sales/Account team early on and keep them engaged during the initiation and planning phases of the project, they will have a lot of background information on the customer's requirements which can help you to better prepare for kick-off and deliver your project

Your plan is only as good as the next two

weeks

At the start of the project you may be asked for a Project Plan that covers the duration and scope of the project, including resources, milestones, etc. Now, this is not an unreasonable request and as a Project Manager you should be able to create a Project Plan – even if it is high-level

One thing to remember though and something I go by, normally your plan is only as good as the next two weeks, four at the most. I would create a plan at a high level for the whole project and a detailed level plan for the next two-four weeks

This provides you with a view of the upcoming tasks and allows for more control

The high-level end-to-end plan should at the very least include the major milestones for the entire project, e.g. Initiation, Design, Implementation, Test, Handover, Closure, etc and these should be planned carefully.

Normally if my major milestones do not change,
I am less concerned about the minor tasks
(slippage) beneath the major milestones

ROUNDING UP THE

HERD

Treat the customer as a friend who might

become an enemy

A great quote to remember is "Give your enemy a thousand chances to become your friend, but never give your friend a single chance to become your enemy"

This is true of your project stakeholders. Always work on building bridges and try to avoid situations that will upset the customer

Bear in mind the customer is not your "friend", despite how well you manage your stakeholders, they are your "customer"

But treating the customer with respect and building relationships will greatly increase the chances of your project being successful and more importantly less escalations when things go wrong – oh and then having a friend at the end of the project!!

Be firm…but build bridges

In the same vein, you need to be firm, but do not burn bridges. Customers will try to walk all over you, it is important from the outset to establish the "rules of engagement".

You may find that customers have formed a pre-project opinion of your company, and it is not always positive – well not from all customer stakeholders

Say, for example, you are on a call and the customer begins to degrade the company you work for.

There are many ways to handle this. For example, if the audience is small, I would say right there and then "we need to try to work together to deliver successfully" in a diplomatic way…. of course

If the audience is large try and find a way to "move on from the contentious topic" and if this is not possible, you may be forced to cut the meeting short and schedule a follow-up call with a "smaller audience"

After the call has finished, you can reach out to the customer and explain that it is not professional to be "thrashing" the company on an open call and if they have issues, you can help to address

If all else fails, time to involve the Account Manager / Account Executive or someone who has a good relationship with the customer, to help re-build bridges

Work for the Customer...accountable to

the Boss

Once I am assigned as a Project Manager to a new project, I usually inform my customer I am "their" project manager and my main focus is foremost, to deliver successfully their objectives

However, keep in mind that you are responsible for delivering project success (customer satisfaction, revenue, margin, etc) to YOUR organisation. You cannot forsake one for the other

It is essential (especially as an external consultant) to become "part of" the customer's team, focused on helping the customer to deliver their objectives, and not simply be seen as an "external contractor/vendor" that is in it for the money

Get closer to difficult stakeholders

Not all project stakeholders will be a supporter of your project and there are often occasions where stakeholders will go out of their way to point out why you or your company should not be delivering the project or look to amplify any little issues into a "major escalation"

As a Project Manager being criticized (personally or the company you work for) on an open call, can be difficult to handle and I know from personal experience, you don't always respond in as a professional manner, as you would when you have had time to "cool down" and think about a response

But it is important that instead of ignoring or giving reasons for the detractors to continue trying to derail your project, you try and find common ground

My approach is to spend more time managing difficult stakeholders, basically DO give them the time of day, try and have one-to-ones with them, "massage" their egos, help them to feel as "important" as they "feel" they are!!

You will find that if you can try to understand their concerns and where they are coming from, it is easier to make them a positive stakeholder, rather than simply pushing back continuously regardless of if they are right or not

The customer is always right – well so they

should be led to believe

Remember, the customer is "ALWAYS" right and so they should always believe. This is a difficult one because you are going to be in situations where you want to *prove* to the customer they are wrong, but this may not always be the smartest move to make

It is *most* of the time better to "allow" the customer to keep the moral high ground, especially when you are knee-deep in delivery and trying to get the project delivered successfully

There are times when you allow the customer to get away with murder and they will still not be a happy customer and complain and complain. I find the best course of action is to try and find common ground and work towards achieving this with the customer

In one example I joined a project where there were multiple delays, the customer blamed us, and we blamed the customer, and mainly it was the customer's fault. There was a lot of talk of ending the contract, fees for re-work, etc, etc. There was dis-harmony in the teams

We got the project back on track by agreeing not to stick too rigidly to the legal terms of the contract, we wouldn't blame/charge the customer for delays and the teams would work as "one team" to deliver the project, we all worked to the same outcome

The customer was not right, but we allowed them to be, and this brought about harmony and a one-team attitude

The Customer WILL have bad days too….

We all have bad days, normally as a result of an external factor (personal, work, etc) and this does impact our work-day and how we interact/respond to trivial issues, that on other days would be a mere blip on the radar

If you have a customer who for no reason or unexpectedly reacts aggressively to what seems like a minor issue, remember they are human and can be having a bad day, which has nothing to do with you or how you are managing the project…. you are just unlucky to bear the brunt of it

As the Project Manager, you should understand the temperature of your project and stakeholders and know when it is better to "stay quiet" and "take it full barrels" from the customer, knowing that it is just a passing phase.

Weather the storm and stay professional, you will find a lot of the time, a good customer will approach you after the event to "apologise"

I will get back to you on that one

You may be on a call with the customer are put in a position where the customer is asking you for a decision or to commit to something that you are not in a position to do at that time OR even have the authority to make the decision

My motto is NEVER saying "NO" to the customer, that is like waving a red flag to a bull. A better response is "Can I take that away and get back to you later today", it's an alternative way of saying "Nope…but let me double-check!!!!". It is sometimes better if the customer is told "no" by someone else in your company

Also, try not to say you are not authorized to make the decision, that usually results in the call ending early – i.e., the customer hanging up and ringing your boss/Account Executive/etc. Better to say you need a little time to review/think about it before giving an answer and then going away and speaking to the decision-makers

COUNTING THE SCUDS

Profit over Customer Satisfaction

All too often I have seen Project Managers who will prioritise making a 100% profit over customer satisfaction. Their focus is on making the planned revenue/margin rather than ensuring that at the end of the project, they have a satisfied customer

Don't get me wrong it is important to bring in planned revenue and make your company the revenue it has forecasted, but a satisfied customer which will result in repeat business is more important to your company

Don't be too quick to stick rigidly to budget at the expense of upsetting the customer, you have contingency and authority to make decisions within your "scope of influence", instead of sticking to the budget

Change Requests – A chance to build

customer relationships

In the same view, change requests are common within all projects (as a reminder, when should you raise a change request? Anytime there is any change to the project even if it is zero cost) – Your ONLY formal PM training in this book!!!

However too many times I have seen PMs very keen to pass on the costs of a change request to the customer, forgetting that they have contingency in their budget or that having a satisfied customer is more important to your organization than making a few extra pennies

As a PM you need to weigh up all aspects of the impact of the change request and then decide on the best course of action. Remember "YOUR" company believes in you so much, they are TRUSTING you to deliver successfully and keep the company afloat – see aren't we important!!!

Once I was managing a project where the customer had delayed the project by six weeks. It would have been easy to raise a change request for the six weeks against the customer, but as a company, we knew that this would upset the customer

What we decided to do was compromise, as a company we were able to bear some of the cost of the delay and still make a good margin on the project, so we agreed with the customer that we would share the impact of the delay. A satisfied customer and the company survived!!!

SET-TO'S – HOW TO

MANAGE

Managing Staff Conflicts

I was once managing a project and I had two software developers who got into a disagreement and asked me to mediate.

My first mistake was not separating both resources and speaking with each on a one-to-one basis, instead, I took both into a meeting room and asked what went wrong.
What a mistake that was, I then spent the next 30 minutes acting like the UN between two warring parties!!! The meeting ended with them being more upset than before

Lesson learned, separate and conquer. If you find yourself in this position, take the heat out of the situation by trying to first speak to the parties individually and try to find the common goal

Once you have your solution, then bring them together, try to move on from the issue and not dwell too much on the root cause – that can be handled at a later time

Use project polls to engage stakeholders

I have joined many projects where members of the project team (Client and Customer) do not understand the objectives, deliverables and outcomes of the project.

One method I have used at the start and then periodically throughout the project is a "project poll" – this can be to an individual email to all stakeholders or if appropriate in a CheckPoint meeting

During the weekly CheckPoint meeting, I would ask everyone to answer a few simple questions which are scored out of 10. For example?

1. Do you understand the objective of the project?

2. Do you know the expected outcomes?

3. Do you understand your role in the project?

4. On a scale of 1 to 10, how involved do you feel?

If the scores are not increasing the longer you are running the project, then you need to figure out why, do you have the correct stakeholders? Communicating effectively? Is the project scope fully understood and correct? etc

Little issues don't matter if you deliver

successfully

During the running of your project, you will come across issues that at the time seem like a major hurdle, often based on the "temperature" of your project, little issues that on other occasions will not matter, can cause your stakeholders to act "irrationally"

One thing to remember is that no one will dwell on "small issues" that occurred during the project if you deliver a successful outcome and the customer and your organization is happy

I have managed many projects where it seemed that the whole world was crumbling and nothing was going right, but communicate, communicate, communicate, and ensure that you keep everyone informed – think of the end game and deliver successfully

Once the project is completed, you will be remembered for delivering successfully, not that minor issue that caused you so many sleepless nights

Manage within your sphere of influence –

escalate

One of the common mistakes I have seen with many Project Managers is that they fail to escalate or handoff issues to the correct stakeholders

I once attended a training course where the trainer spoke to us about not worrying about things that were outside the sphere of our influence

So, for example, if you are driving to work and there is a traffic jam, there is absolutely nothing you can do about it, so why worry and get yourself upset

The same principle applies to Project Management, if the issue is outside of your scope of influence to resolve, then escalate to the correct level.

There is no point in trying to own an issue that you cannot resolve, an important skill of a PM is knowing when you escalate and to whom

Don't present issues without options

Have you ever been in a situation where you have gone to your boss (at work or home!!!) with an issue and the boss's response is "what are you going to do about it"

Let's say your better half arrives home from a long day's work and you meet them at the door with the news "We have run out of wine!" I think the response would be "And…what are you doing about it?"

A much better scenario is "We have run out of wine, but I have ordered via delivery or we have Gin". Now you have given options and the response will hopefully be much better

Always be prepared. When I first became a
Project Manager, my manager gave me some
very good advice, he said to me, never to present
issues to senior stakeholders without having at
least two options to resolve the issue you are
presenting

This is also even more pertinent if you are
informing the customer of an issue. For example,
late delivery of hardware. Have some options,
e.g. partial implementation, making use of
existing hardware, order alternatives, etc

By the way, if you "run out of wine", that is poor
planning on your behalf…. but that's another
lesson

It will be better tomorrow

"It will be better tomorrow", is one of my life's
mottos and it does help me to get through some
of the "bad times"

Sometimes it is really difficult to see the light at
the end of the tunnel and even if you can see the
light determine if it is an oncoming train or
indeed the light at the end of the tunnel

Keep looking ahead. As bad as things look in the moment, if you follow your methodology, keep delivering, and don't allow the minor setbacks to de-rail you (see that I did there!!!) then you can always look to tomorrow (even if THAT tomorrow is 6 months in the future)

Don't let minor issues distract you from

the end goal

I have known a lot of Project Managers who come to me regarding minor issues (e.g. having to assign a resource for an extra day that was not budgeted for, or the customer asking for an additional feature that will result in minor additional costs to the organization)

Now as a PM (*who your company has empowered*), you need to be able to determine what you can accept and what you need to seek advice for, but at the end of the day, if you deliver a successful project, a satisfied customer, and repeat business, then it would be a pretty bad boss who castigates you for going over budget slightly or being slightly late on a deliverable

Never send the first e-mail draft

I have done this many times. You received an email from someone which includes contents that you don't agree with or you perceive that it is questioning your ability and you respond while upset

I have learned over time not to be too quick to respond and it is best to re-read the email and re-write (many times) it when you have calmed down a bit. Be careful of your language and never respond in the heat of the moment

A tip is to remove the recipients while "ranting", so there is no chance of accidentally sending the email

Never send the first draft!!

Call first…then send an e-mail

I usually find that if there is a contentious topic or disagreement with the customer, that it is better to have a call or face-to-face conversation before sending an email. This is also true for internal stakeholders – it's good to talk!!

Everyone interprets (tone and content) an e-mail differently, and you won't always get your points across in the manner and understanding in which you hoped you would

Having a call and discussing first, always helps and can help to remove any "problems" between you and the customer

But then send THAT email, to summarize what was discussed and agreed. Keep a record

It is sometimes better not to respond

Sometimes it is better not to respond to some emails, especially if you find the participants are getting more and more upset or the sender of the email is not such an "influential" stakeholder!!!

Sometimes responding only results in more unnecessary emails and possible escalations and simply ignoring the email or responding with something along the lines of "OK, I understand, can we pick this up on our next call" is better than trying to respond back to every "point" made in the email – this is also good advice for your "personal" conversations

But if you do find that some stakeholders are constantly barraging you with "unnecessary emails" – See "Get closer to difficult stakeholders"!!

THE CATTLE DRIVE

Many bosses within the same organization

Have you ever been running a project and had too many bosses, i.e. the Account Team, your manager, the customer, the sales team, etc?

The main thing is to ensure you understand your stakeholder's needs and can communicate effectively

If possible, identify your "major" stakeholder (your Senior User or Supplier) and ensure you engage early in the project – this will help to ensure that they support you on calls and in decision-making

Ensure reports are distributed to the correct audience. You will find that a lot of the time, the reason so many people are wanting to "stick" their "Nose" in, is because they are not aware of what progress is being made, they want confidence that the project is being delivered properly and the customer is happy

Communicate, Communicate, Communicate

The worst thing you can do is not communicate.

Sometimes a PM will not communicate with their stakeholders (especially if the project is on hold or there has been no progress), or even worst, they ONLY have bad news

Even if there has been no progress, continuing to communicate to your stakeholders (especially the client) helps to reassure the client that they have not been forgotten and will help to prevent any complaints about lack of engagement

Send out the report/e-mail that states "No further progress this week, will update next week…", etc, the customer is kept informed and lines of communication kept open

IF there is ONLY bad news, see "Don't present issues without options"

AROUND THE

CAMPFIRE

Be ready for your meetings

As a general rule please don't schedule a meeting and turn up without preparing for it

For one it will be difficult to stick to the agenda (see below) and number two it will help you achieve the objectives of the meeting

I always say, let's not start the meeting with a blank piece of paper and as such, I would either prepare a few slides or send out in advance of the meeting the material I am looking to discuss

Another tip, it is always better to schedule a call with internal stakeholders before getting on a call with the customer, especially where there has been as customer escalation

Ensure that before you speak to the customer, all internal stakeholders are on the same page and you have agreed who will take the lead and handle specific topics on the call

You will never stick to the agenda

First and foremost, always add an agenda to your meeting invites. Too often I have seen meeting invites sent out without an agenda. I have known stakeholders who will refuse to attend a meeting without an agenda

Secondly, you will never stick to the agenda, well not without controlling the meeting

Try your best to keep participants on topic and not to stray, but this is easier said than done

Sometimes though having an open discussion is beneficial and knowing when to let the conversation "ramble" on and when to cut in to bring the conversation back to the agenda topic is an important skill to have…and learned over many years of experience and upsetting people

However, be aware of those attendees that try to take over the meeting and over-discuss points (excluding the majority of the attendees) that really should be taken out of the meeting. Try to head these off early

Remember this is *your* meeting (*you are empowered*) and there is nothing wrong with saying, "that we need to get back to the agenda" and suggesting a follow-up meeting for any other topics that were not on the agenda

Sometimes though, despite your best efforts, you WILL have meetings that discussed everything, other than what was on your agenda – *It will be better tomorrow*!!!

Listen to your audience

By this I do not mean to what they are saying, but more importantly to what they are not saying

If for example you have made a really important point on a call or one of your SMEs has spent "ages" explaining a key design concept and at the end there is no comment, then especially if you are not face to face, it can be difficult to know if they agree or the point just got lost in translation

Don't just move on with the agenda, take time to ask the attendees *"if they had any questions?"* or more importantly *"is there anyone who would like a bit more clarification?"*

Recap meetings

To be honest, I don't always do this, but I tend to do it when there were important decisions made or where there was a meeting to discuss urgent project issues/escalations and we have agreed on the next actions or when I want to reinforce points agreed in the meeting

At the end of the meeting, recap the main points and actions agreed upon, ask if you have missed any important points, and then remember to send out the meeting minutes

Send out Meeting Minutes

As mentioned above, capture and send out meeting minutes. I don't subscribe to the process of writing down everything that was said in the meeting (verbatim), to be honest, if you need to do that, record the meeting

© William Layne, 2023

Instead capture any key points, decisions, and follow-up actions. Ensure the minutes include the attendees and those who were invited but did not attend. It is important to have this so that if in the future there is disagreement on any points, you can go back to the recorded minutes

I always include a sentence such as "Please let me know if you disagree or require any changes to these minutes", that way you are implicitly asking for approval of the minutes

Also please don't forget to send out the minutes!!!!

Keep track of key decisions

So, you are running a meeting and a key decision is made…but you did not minute it or record it in a decision log. Remember if it is not written down…it didn't happen. Everyone remembers conversations in a different way to suit their agendas – we all know that from personal and bitter experiences

Record key decisions and minutes and then distribute the minutes, you do not need the

customer to respond to be able to have the
"proof" of what was said or agreed in the past

p.s. don't start recording your "personal"
decisions with your partner – that is NOT what I
am saying!!!

Don't be too quick to own actions

I have been to a lot of meetings where the chair
of the meeting (or Project Manager) is very quick
to own actions, usually as no one else steps
forward to own the action

I have always said that the sign of a well-run
meeting, is when I come away with no actions.

If at the end of the meeting actions are assigned,
that means you invited the right stakeholders and
assigned the actions to the best person to deal
with the actions

Take ownership of "project" problems

During projects, issues may occur which are not
directly related to your project, but may impact

the "customers" wider scope of work (e.g. hardware support)

Ensure you are aware of these and can involve the correct parties / report on the issues where appropriate

There is nothing worst than being asked about a project issue (that is seen as important and relevant) by your customer and not being aware of it or being able to escalate to the correct person to answer

Remember "you need to be that person that people are happy to approach". *Be empowered*!!!

THE GUNFIGHT

Resources booking full-time - but should

be part-time

It is important that you track the effort of resources assigned to your project – especially what they are booking versus what was assigned/being used

Remember this is "cost" against your project and will affect your gross margin/profit

Be wary of resources who assume once assigned believe they can book full time to your project, even though they are not 100 percent assigned or not doing actual work

One method I use on larger projects when resources are assigned is to send out an email with the expected duration of the project, key deliverables, and effort that should be booked

You could also send out weekly e-mails (similar to Work Packages in P2) outlining what is expected of each resource. This also means that

"You" as the Project Manager has spent time reviewing your plan!!!

Be confident…even with technical teams

There is nothing worse than sitting on a call as the Project Manager and not being able to understand or keep track of decisions being made. I am not saying you need to have detailed technical knowledge – NO, but you should be able to understand sufficiently to be able to be in a position to make decisions

As a Project Manager, you need to be confident when managing your technical stakeholders, this not only builds confidence that the SMEs would have in you but also allows you as a PM to "challenge" some of the decisions being made by the technical team – See Technical SMEs focus below!!!

If required, before the main call/meeting, meet with your SMEs to get a better understanding of the topics to be discussed, one of my favorite quotes to Technical SMEs is "can you explain that to me in English (or Project Management spiel) please?"

Most technical SMEs will be very pleased to spend time with you as they will know if you understand where they are coming from, you are more likely to support their decisions

Technical SMEs focus on Scope and

Quality...PMs don't

I was once assigned as a Program Manager on a program where the company I worked for under-bid the competition to be able to win the deal – they were looking to get into the industry and were looking for a "reference site"

The program was underpriced and under-resourced, the scope was not confirmed but was fixed-price, with a fixed outcome – but we were STILL expected to make a "profit"

Even in this scenario, the Senior Solution Architect (a very good friend of mine!!) focused more on the scope and quality of the deliverables – which is natural, rather than delivering an "acceptable" outcome for the customer

As a Project Manager, whether you like it or not, Price and Time are more important factors to us, we want to deliver on time and within budget

You need to work closely with your technical SMEs to help define an "acceptable" acceptance criteria/quality threshold for deliverables - Set expectations early on with technical SMEs in terms of effort and deliverable dates

Given a chance, a GOOD technical SME will never want to release a document until they are 110 percent completed with it – sometimes projects just don't have the luxury for this. Be pragmatic, but do not release sub-standard deliverables, look for opportunities for partial / draft releases that will help dependent activities to begin, change the format of deliverables (e.g. Excel instead of Word), SMEs write less in Excel documents, etc, etc

Don't have technical conversations without your SME present

Please try not to have technical conversations with the customer without your relevant technical SMEs available. If you think you are going into a call where the customer is going to get technical, ask for technical support. If all else fails, well "Can I get back to you later on that point….."

Engineers WILL complain

They just do…. they are never happy. Remember your "people management" skills. Listen to them and in all honesty, if there is something you can do that will make them know you are listening, they will become your friend for life and will go the extra mile for you

Don't argue in-front of the customer

Try your best not to have disagreements with your own team in front of the customer, this not only makes you and your company look bad, it reduces confidence the customer has in you to manage the project

If you do find that on a call / in a meeting you are disagreeing with your team, if possible send a "Teams" message to the member of your team with a "subtle" message, maybe "can we end this conversation and have a chat later please". You will find that if you have an internal meeting with your team to agree agenda and what is being discussed before speaking to the customer, the chances of disagreeing is greatly reduced

If it is in an in-person meeting that you find yourself disagreeing, then depending on the topic, it may be best to ignore it and pick it up after the customer meeting has ended

You will learn more from difficult projects

As a new PM, don't be too concerned about difficult projects (i.e. those with many issues or those that fail). They say you learn from your mistakes, and the key point here is that "*you learn from your mistakes*"

Despite all of your planning and coordination, there are always issues which will arise in a project, but if you can overcome these and gather

and act on lessons learned, it will make you a
better and more confident project manager

TOMBSTONE

What's the famous grave in Tombstone..." Here lies Lester Moore, shot four times from a forty-four, No Less, No More"

Projects rarely run smoothly, challenging meetings, SMEs have not delivered, the SoW is vague and you don't have enough resources, etc, etc

But remember Project Management is about delivering output and change, and change is rarely easy to accept. Be confident, prepare, and be ready to do battle with all that comes – but battle with a smile and respect

Try not to dwell too much on the bumps along the way, keep focusing on the end goal and delivering a successful outcome

Anyone can be a Project Manager, but not every Project Manager will have the people skills required to be able to successfully deliver projects and ensure all stakeholders are happy.

Go forth and deliver......*Be Empowered*

© William Layne, 2023

www.ingramcontent.com/pod-product-compliance
Lightning Source LLC
Chambersburg PA
CBHW071115220526
45467CB00004B/1887